The Marshmallow Family

Loving From the Heart

Written by Tammy Williams

The Marshmallow Family

Sharing a Story of *Love* Through Pictures

Written by Tammy Williams

© 2014 by Tammy Williams.
All rights reserved. No part of this book may be reproduced, stored in a retrieval system or transmitted in any form or by any means without the prior written permission of the publishers, except by a reviewer who may quote brief passages in a review to be printed in a newspaper, magazine or journal.

First Printing

Revival Waves of Glory Books & Publishing has allowed this work to remain exactly as the author intended, verbatim, without editorial input.

Ebook 978-1-312-10148-7
Softcover 978-1-312-10143-2
Hardcover 978-1-312-10412-9

PUBLISHED BY REVIVAL WAVES OF GLORY BOOKS & PUBLISHING
www.revivalwavesofgloryministries.com
Litchfield, IL

Printed in the United States of America

Dedication

This Book is dedicated to my Wonderful and Loving Children

Corey, Taylon, and Lauren

Mommy Loves You All!!

Welcome to the Town Of Mallow Creek

In the town of Mallow Creek lived loving, soft and cuddly families made of colorful marshmallows. These families were like none ever seen before and they looked different from people. All the marshmallow families loved to love and never heard of any words that were mean or hurtful. The town was always fun and exciting and everyone got along. Throughout the day the kids would play together and bounce their soft bodies around as if on a trampoline. While their parents walked around the neighborhood laughing and talking with everyone in sight. The families enjoyed getting together to share pictures and telling exciting stories.

The temperature was always cool and pleasant just perfect for their gentle bodies. The sky was blue, the sun bright and the stars shined like diamonds at night. Their homes were made of pine wood, and the yard was full of the greenest grass, with trees that swayed with the calm and relaxing breeze. The town was so clean that you could eat off the ground and so peaceful that you could sleep outside.

The Mallow Creek families were known for giving hugs and made sure no one ever went unnoticed or unloved. They didn't need much of anything to survive because everything they needed was stored in their hearts. Hugs and sweet words flowed from family to family throughout the day and night and peaceful dreams awaited them as they slept.

On a brisk and calm morning, Momma Sarah Marshabe was in her front yard watering her bright colorful flowers. As she reached to grab her watering pot, she noticed a man with his wife and four children riding along on a big bike. The bike had a basket in the back filled with their precious belongings.

"Good Morning Lovely Family! What a delightful day." greeted Sarah. But the family kept right on riding. "Oh maybe they didn't hear me, I'll be sure to give each one of them a big hug the next time I see them" said Sarah as she continued to water her flowers.

Martha Walsh who lived next door to the Marshabe's came out of house with great excitement shouting out to Sarah "Did you see the new family that just moved into town? They're moving in the old Marshbocks farmhouse!"

"Oh yes!! I greeted them but they didn't hear me. It's always wonderful having new families move into town. More love and hugs to share. Hooray!! Maybe we should make a couple of desserts and take to them." suggested Sarah.

"Sure thing"! Martha replied. "I'll make them my grandmother's Hugalot berry pie. They'll love it!"

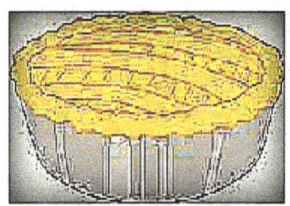 

"And I'll make my Joy pudding, that will put a smile on their faces." said Sarah. "I'll see you in a bit Martha."

Later that day Sarah and Martha got their desserts together and with great excitement walked quickly to greet the new family at their home.

Sarah rang the doorbell. But there was no answer as they stood at the door patiently. Suddenly they heard a creek as the door slowly opened, but no one was there.

"Well Hello!" said Sarah, as she looked down to greet the tiny Mulberry family. "Welcome to Mallow Creek! My name is Sarah Marshabe and this is my dear friend Martha Walsh. We just wanted to stop by and send our warmest welcome along with a couple of baked goods to say we love you!" But the Mulberry family showed no excitement.

Martha then handed Mrs. Mulberry her hugalot berry pie along with a bit a family history behind it. "My grandma Ruby made this pudding as a way to give pies and hugs at the same time." The family stood at the door looking puzzled. Mr. Mulberry thanked them for the desserts and slammed the door.

"Have a great day"! shouted Sarah loud enough so that the family could hear her through the door.

"They must have been busy putting away their things we'll come back another day for the hugs!"

"That sounds delightful!" said Martha. "A big hug always gets my heart pumping with love."

Sarah quickly went home to tell Papa Don Marshabe and their kids the great news. "Hello Papa, what a great day in Mallow Creek!"

"Yes it is Dear, the air has an extra pop of love in

it today." said Papa.

"It surely does! But what's even more wonderful is that we have a new family to love. They just moved into the old Marshembocks farmhouse so Martha Walsh and I cooked our favorite desserts and took them to the family to express how happy we are to have them." Sarah explained.

"What a thoughtful gift! I know they were happy too!" said Papa.

"I'm sure they were, but they seemed to be in a great hurry so they didn't have time to really say anything but Thank you." Sarah said.

"Really." said Papa. I wonder why, the people in this town can talk for days without taking a breath especially when they're really excited. Maybe we should find out more about them and where they're from. This way we will better understand what they need from us through love. Everyone shows love in different ways, but when it's from the heart there's a special kind of feeling."

"I think we should do something very special. How about we have a welcome picnic so that the entire town will be able to greet them." suggested Sarah.

"Great idea! the kids and I will walk down to their farmhouse to introduce ourselves and then invite them. This is going to be so much fun." said Papa.

As Papa and the children got closer to the Mulberry farmhouse, they noticed Mr. Mulberry in the yard. He was very tiny with a beard and streaks of gray hair. Papa walked up to him and introduced himself.

"Hello, my name is Papa Marshabe but you can call me Don and these here are my children Bouncer, and Patience."

With his head down low and in a shy voice Mr. Mulberry introduced his family, all of whom were very tiny and different than the other marshmallow families.

"Hi I'm Bobby, this is my wife Grace and our children Jane, Janet, Jamie, and James."

"It's very nice to meet you all. We are so happy and excited that your family has moved to Mallow Creek. Whenever we get new families in our town, we have a huge picnic to honor their arrival. We want to set it up for tomorrow so that everyone in town will have a chance to get to know your family." said Papa.

"Thank you, but we are not interested." said Mr. Mulberry. He then turned away and walked in the house as his tiny family followed.

Papa and the children stood silently and watched as the family went into the house. They then turned and walked back home, but they didn't feel their normal happy way. They began to have a sad weird feeling something they had never felt before.

When Papa got home he went to Sarah and said "Tomorrow we will have the entire town meet at the Mulberry's home to sing a song of happiness and love until they come out. Then we will shower them with love letters, cards and gifts. We will not give up until they feel the love of the town."

"Another great idea Papa! Love shouldn't ever stop even if the other person doesn't feel the same way. We will continue to show them love and soon it will feel so good to them, they will want to love back." said Sarah.

"You're right dear!" said Papa. "Well, let's get some sleep we have a long day ahead of us."

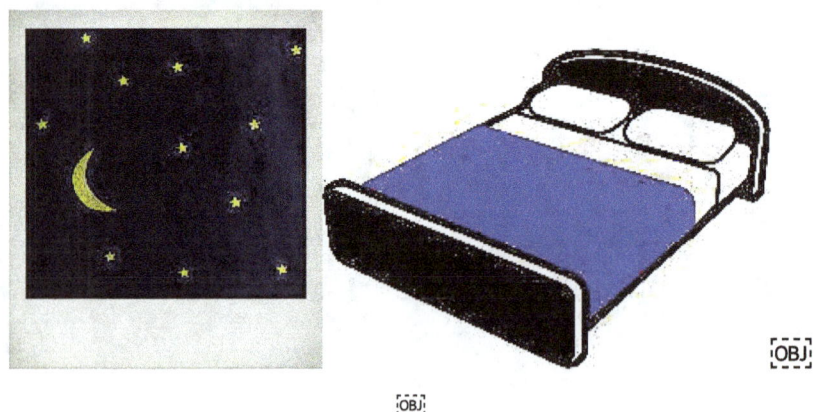

The next morning, news had spread throughout the entire town to meet at the Mulberry's farmhouse. There were families everywhere ready to share their love. As the crowd grew bigger, the Mulberry's farmhouse became completely surrounded with the town's love. "Let's sing the Greatest Heart song" shouted one of the children in the crowd.

The crowd began to sing……...

"The greatest heart is the one from within it has no hate only love to the end you can try to stop it but it starts all over again because the greatest heart only knows love from within."

As the song is being sung Mr. Mulberry stuck his head out the door and slowly walked on the porch. "Wow! he said. What's going on?"

"This is our way of saying welcome and we love your family." shouted a crowd member.

"We've never felt this kind of love. In the town we're from everyone mistreated us and ran us away because we looked different. It's a great feeling to know people love us even though we don't look like the other families!" said Mr. Mulberry.

"We are all unique in our own way that's why loving is so exciting and fun. Being different is great, it is what makes us who we are." said Sarah.

Soon the entire Mulberry family was standing on the porch with tears of joy and excitement. They began to thank everyone for their support and kindness as they walked through the crowd shaking hands and hugging everyone.

Songs of love continued to spread a joyful cheer.

The Mulberry family began to meet and make new friends. The kids played with other kids while their parents talked and laughed with the adults. They learned that everyone is different, but love should be the same in every heart. And no matter how big or small, love always remains
Tall.

www.ingramcontent.com/pod-product-compliance
Lightning Source LLC
Chambersburg PA
CBHW072116290426
44110CB00014B/1935